The Role of Women In Imām al-Ḥusayn's Uprising

Ayatullāh Shahīd Sayyid Muḥammad Baqir al-Hakim قدس سره

AL-BURĀQ
Heighten The Mind

Copyright

ISBN: 978-1-956276-00-8

Translated and annotated by al-Burāq Publications. Where needed, context and transliterations were added.
Printed and published by al-Burāq Publications.

Ordering Information
We offer discounts and promotions for wholesale purchases and for non-profit organizations, libraries, and other educational institutions. Contact us at the email below for further information.

www.al-Buraq.org
publications@al-Buraq.org

First printed edition | August 2021
Second printed edition | January 2022

Dedication

The publication of this book was made possible through the generous support of our donors.

بِسْمِ ٱللَّهِ ٱلرَّحْمَٰنِ ٱلرَّحِيمِ
ٱلْحَمْدُ لِلَّهِ رَبِّ ٱلْعَٰلَمِينَ ٱلرَّحْمَٰنِ ٱلرَّحِيمِ
مَٰلِكِ يَوْمِ ٱلدِّينِ إِيَّاكَ نَعْبُدُ وَإِيَّاكَ نَسْتَعِينُ
ٱهْدِنَا ٱلصِّرَٰطَ ٱلْمُسْتَقِيمَ صِرَٰطَ ٱلَّذِينَ
أَنْعَمْتَ عَلَيْهِمْ غَيْرِ ٱلْمَغْضُوبِ عَلَيْهِمْ
وَلَا ٱلضَّآلِّينَ

Please recite *Sūrah al-Fātiha* and ask Allāh for the Divine reward (*thawāb*) to be conferred upon the donors and also the souls of all the deceased in whose memory their loved ones have contributed graciously towards the publication of *The Role of Women In Imām al-Ḥusayn's Uprising.*

We want to begin by giving all praise and thanks to Allah ﷻ for giving us the tawfiq to translate this book. He has guided us and without Him, we would not have been guided to the straight path embodied by the Prophet Muḥammad ﷺ and the Ahl al-Bayt عليهم السلام.

This book is dedicated firstly to Ayatullāh Shahīd Sayyid Muḥammad Baqir al-Hakim قدس سره, who made tremendous strides in advancing the cause of Islam. It is also dedicated to all the scholars, martyrs and believers who worked tirelessly to promote the pure Muḥammadan path.

We want to also give our thanks and appreciation to all believers from around the world and acknowledge the team which helped al-Burāq Publications complete this work, spending countless hours to make its publication possible. Please recite Sūrah al-Fātiḥah on behalf of them and their marhūmēn.

This book is dedicated in honor of the following individuals. Please remember them in your prayers and may Allah ﷻ have mercy on them and their loved ones.

Abdul Hussen Amin Saad

Ahmad Ali Amen Shryim

Ali Ahmed Ftouni

Ali Baydoun

Marhūmēn and shuhada' of Millat e Jaffariya

Alya Victoria Agemy Yazback

Amin Bakri

Darlene Joanne Hammond

Fatima Bai

Fatima Mohessin

Fatima Noureddine

Fatima Salameh

Georgi Abass Talevski

Gulistan Ali NasrAllah

Habib Saleh

Hajj Abdul Hassan Fakih

Hajj Abdul-Amir Mroue

Hajj Ali Akil Issa

Hajj Ali Youssef Amin Dabaja

Hajj Ali Zeitoun

Hajj Hassan Mahmoud Sobh

Hajj Mohamad El-sayed Allam

Hajj Youssef Dabaja

Hajji Amneh Mahmoud Sobh-Ftouni

Hajji Ghani Hassani

Hajji Iman Elsaghir

Hajji Mariam Serhan

Hajji Sabah Kanso

Hajji Siham Fawaz-Wazne

Hajji Zahra Slieman-Aoun

Hassan Khalil Baydoun

Hussein Ahmad Ghasham

Inayat Fatima

Jaasmiya Al-Sunaid

Laila Begum

Mahmoud Tiba

Mahmoud Zahr

Mohammed Husain Jafri

Muhammad Makki

Munib Baydoun

Najibeh Baydoun

Nasar Makki

Nazih Kassem Baydoun

Turfah Kassem Sobh

Zeinab Baydoun

Duaa al-Hujja

اللهم كن لوليك الحجة بن الحسن صلواتك
عليه وعلى آبائه في هذه الساعة وفي كل
ساعة وليا وحافظا وقائدا وناصرا ودليلا
وعينا حتى تسكنه أرضك طوعا وتمتعه فيها طويلا

O Allah, be, for Your representative, the Hujjat (proof), son of al-Hasan, Your blessings be upon him and his forefathers, in this hour and in every hour: a guardian, a protector, a leader, a helper, a proof, and an eye - until You make him live on the Earth, in obedience (to You), and cause him to live in it for a long time.

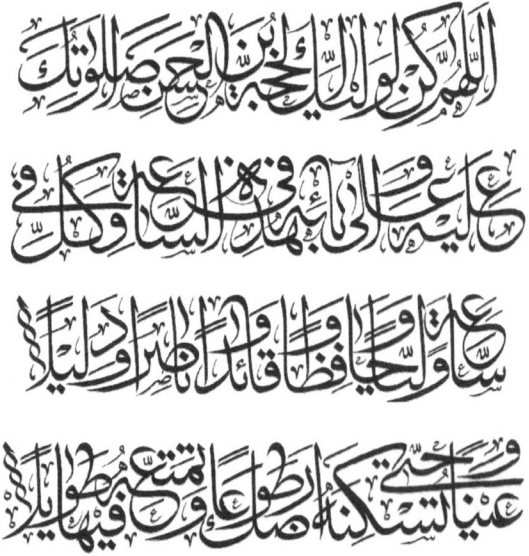

Terms of Respect

The following Arabic phrases have been used throughout this book in their respective places to show the reverence which the noble personalities deserve.

عزّ وجلّ

Used for Allāh (God) meaning:
Exalted and Sublime (Perfect) is He

صلى الله عليه وآله وسلم

Used for Prophet Muḥammad meaning:
Blessings from Allāh be upon him and his family

عليه السلام

Used for a man of high status (singular) meaning:
Peace be upon him

عليها السلام

Used for woman of a high status (singular) meaning:
Peace be upon her

عليهما السلام

Used for men/women of a high status (dual) meaning:
Peace be upon them both

عليهم السلام

Used for men and/or women of a high status (plural) meaning:
Peace be upon them all

قدس سره

Used for a deceased scholar meaning:
May his resting [burial] place remain pure

Transliteration Table

The method of transliteration of Islamic terminology from the Arabic language has been carried out according to the standard transliteration table below.

ء	ʾ	ر	r	ف	f
ا	a	ز	z	ق	q
ب	b	س	s	ك	k
ت	t	ش	sh	ل	l
ث	th	ص	ṣ	م	m
ج	j	ض	ḍ	ن	n
ح	ḥ	ط	ṭ	و	w
خ	kh	ظ	ẓ	ه	h
د	d	ع	ʿ	ي	y
ذ	dh	غ	gh		
		Long Vowels			
ا	ā	و	ū	ي	ī
		Short Vowels			
ـَ	a	ـُ	u	ـِ	i

Terms of Respect

The following Arabic phrases have been used throughout this book in their respective places to show the reverence which the noble personalities deserve.

عزّ وجلّ

Used for Allāh (God) meaning:
Exalted and Sublime (Perfect) is He

صلى الله عليه وآله

Used for Prophet Muḥammad meaning:
Blessings from Allāh be upon him and his family

عليه السلام

Used for a man of high status (singular) meaning:
Peace be upon him

عليها السلام

Used for woman of a high status (singular) meaning:
Peace be upon her

عليهما السلام

Used for men/women of a high status (dual) meaning:
Peace be upon them both

عليهم السلام

Used for men and/or women of a high status (plural) meaning:
Peace be upon them all

قدس سره

Used for a deceased scholar meaning:
May his resting [burial] place remain pure

Transliteration Table

The method of transliteration of Islamic terminology from the Arabic language has been carried out according to the standard transliteration table below.

ء	ʾ	ر	r	ف	f
ا	a	ز	z	ق	q
ب	b	س	s	ك	k
ت	t	ش	sh	ل	l
ث	th	ص	ṣ	م	m
ج	j	ض	ḍ	ن	n
ح	ḥ	ط	ṭ	و	w
خ	kh	ظ	ẓ	ه	h
د	d	ع	ʿ	ي	y
ذ	dh	غ	gh		
Long Vowels					
ا	ā	و	ū	ي	ī
Short Vowels					
ـَ	a	ـُ	u	ـِ	i

Table of Contents

About the Author 1

Preface 5

Fighting in Allah's Way 13

Preserving the Virtuous Remnant (al-Baqiyya al-Ṣāliḥa) 23

Preserving Values and Morals 35

The Role of Publicity 51

- The Importance of Publicity in Politics 51
- Publicizing the Ḥusaynī Uprising 53
- Publicity in the Political Sphere 60

Captivity 67

About the Author

Ayatullāh Shahīd Sayyid Muḥammad Baqir al-Hakim قدس سره was a Shia marja', jurist and revolutionary scholar. He was the head, and a founder, of the Islamic Supreme Council of Iraq and also a founder of the Islamic Da'wa Party, and fought the ruling Ba'ath Party in Iraq for decades. He was the fifth son of Shia marjja' Ayatullāh al-Sayyid Muhsin al-Hakim. He was born in Najaf on August 12, 1939.

Ayatullāh Shahīd Sayyid Muḥammad Baqir al-Hakim studied seminary courses with his father, developed an expertise in philosophy and Qur'ānic sciences, and achieved the degree of ijtihad in Islamic jurisprudence and principles of jurisprudence. He then moved to Baghdad, where he taught Qur'ānic sciences and jurisprudence in Usul al-Din College from 1964 to 1975. He also collaborated in the foundation of the School of Islamic Sciences (*Madrasat al-'Ulum al-Islamiyya*).

Ayatullāh Shahīd Sayyid Muḥammad Baqir al-Hakim was trusted by his father, and participated in many Islamic activities as his father's representative. Together with Sayyid Muḥammad Mahdi al-Hakim, and some others, he founded al-Da'wa Party in 1958, and during the marja'iyya of Sayyid Muḥammad Baqir al-Sadr, he acted under his supervision.

Following increased pressures and the impossibility of political activity in Iraq, Ayatullāh Shahīd Sayyid Muḥammad Baqir al-Hakim departed to Damascus in 1980. He then moved to the Islamic Republic of Iran.

In the Islamic Republic of Iran, he participated in political and cultural activities and undertook a number of positions over the two decades he was there.

In 1999, Ayatullāh Shahīd Sayyid Muḥammad Baqir al-Hakim propounded his view of expertise in religious marja'iyya.

After the American invasion on Iraq and the collapse of the Ba'ath regime in 2003, he returned to Iraq on May 11, 2003 of the same year and resided in Najaf. However, he was martyred on August 29, 2003, in a car bomb attack after his imamate of the Friday Prayer and at the time of leaving the Shrine of Imām Ali عليه السلام.

Preface

بسم الله الرحمن الرحيم

In the Name of Allāh, the Most Gracious, the Most Merciful

Praise be to Allah, Lord of the Worlds, and peace and salutations be upon our master and Prophet, the master of prophets and messengers, the beloved of the Lord of the Worlds, Abū al-Qāsim Muḥammad and his blessed and pure family, and the chosen ones of his companions.

Peace be upon you, O my master Aba-ʿAbdillāh and upon the souls that gathered in your courtyard. Peace of Allah be upon you from me forever, as long as I may live and as long as there is day and night. May Allah not make this my last visit to you all. Peace be upon al-Ḥusayn, and upon ʿAlī b. al-Ḥusayn, and upon the sons of al-Ḥusayn, and upon the companions of al-Ḥusayn.

Peace be on our lord and master, the remnant of Allah in His land, al-Ḥujja b. al-Ḥasan (May Allah hasten his holy reappearance), and peace be on the martyrs of Islam everywhere from the formative period of Islam until this age.

We are currently reliving the memory of the Battle of Karbalāʾ; the memory of the great catastrophe, the major calamity, and the painful tragedy; one that befell the Ahl al-Bayt on the day of ʿAshūrā and the days that preceded and followed it. On days such as these, in Ṣafar, the children, women, and household of the Messenger of Allah, and the last remnants who survived the epic of Karbalāʾ and ʿAshūrā, suffered captivity and sorrow.

In regards to the revolution of Imām al-Ḥusayn, the topic of captivity is one of the significant matters that should be particularly discussed. It is a topic that raises a broader issue that concerns this revolution, i.e. the role of women in the cause of Imām al-Ḥusayn. Despite the virtuous efforts of all of those whom endeavored to discuss and examine the cause of Imām al-Ḥusayn ﷺ — including researchers, speakers, poets, etc.— and the issue of [the women's] captivity, this topic and the role of women in the cause of Imām al-Ḥusayn ﷺ has remained an entirely independent subject in itself—one that requires more study and contemplation. And thus far, it has not received enough attention and assessment as it should, as I will elaborate. These two topics are also very important for our own political and social realities, as they revolve around the role that women can undertake in all ages and generations; Allah ﷻ has ordained this role for women in life and society. Women are one half of human society, and they bear a general responsibility to it as they have a major role in its progression and attainment of perfection.

The Noble Qur'ān also mentioned and asserted this major role, given women's share in human life and society.

This is why when some noble verses draw the example of the faithless and the faithful — clearly, the terms faithless and faithful are not specific to one group of people to the exclusion of others; they are terms referring to all the faithless and all the faithful, be they men, women, young, old, knowledgeable scholars, or rank-and-file commoners—it uses the example of women: "Allah draws an example for the faithless: the wife of Noah and the wife of Lot. They were under two of our righteous servants, yet they betrayed them. So they did not avail them in any way against Allah, and it was said [to them], 'Enter the Fire, along with those who enter [it].'"[1] Here, Allah draws the example of the faithless with these two women, then He draws the example of the faithful with two women, one of whom is Pharaoh's wife: "Allah draws an[other] example for those who have faith: the wife of Pharaoh, when she said, 'My Lord! Build me a home near You in paradise, and deliver me from Pharaoh and his conduct, and deliver me from the wrongdoing lot,'"[2] and the other being Mary daughter of Imran: "And Mary, daughter of Imran, who guarded the chastity of her

---

[1] Sūrat al-Taḥrīm, verse 10.

[2] Sūrat al-Taḥrīm, verse 11.

womb, so We breathed into it of Our spirit. She confirmed the words of her Lord and His Books, and she was one of the obedient."[3]

In addition, highlighting the role of women in the cause of Imām al-Ḥusayn ﷺ sheds light on their role in human society at large, particularly in the public political and social spheres. Women had a commensurately large and important role in the uprising of Imām al-Ḥusayn ﷺ that is not beneath the role of men, especially if we consider the particularities of Imām al-Ḥusayn ﷺ as an Imām who should be obeyed and who possesses unique characteristics that no regular person could equal.

In regard to the battle of Karbalāʾ, martyrdom, ransom, generosity, sacrifice, suffering, and all other things that the Imām and his household and companions who participated in this battle went through, the Imām himself remains the symbol of all these men. As for the women, al-Ḥawrāʾ Zaynab ﷺ, this majestic woman, al-ʿAqīla of Banū Hāshim, is another symbol in this movement.

[3] Sūrat al-Taḥrīm, verse 12.

We notice this role in other members of Imām al-Ḥusayn's ﷺ family, and in a number of other women, each according to her position and status.

The roles, acts, and deeds undertaken in the cause of Imām al-Ḥusayn ﷺ by the women in general, and by al-ʿAqīla (Sayyida Zaynab ﷺ) in particular, may be summarized under five key roles and headings.

Fighting in Allah's Way

The first role is fighting in Allah's ﷻ way, which was the most prominent factor in Imām al-Ḥusayn's عليه السلام movement. We find that women participated in this uprising at the level of the actual battle, although the well-known position of Islam — which was also reiterated in the battle of Karbalāʾ — is that there is no obligation upon women, i.e. they are not obligated to fight. However, it behooves us to consider the following:

Firstly, in the essence of the *Sharia* and its rulings, the obligation of fighting in Allah's ﷻ way sometimes becomes incumbent on women if the fighting and *jihād* are defensive, in the jurists' terms, and if women are able to take part, with the caveat that the number of fighting men is insufficient.

According to the *Sharia*, *jihād* is usually divided into two parts:

1- Preemptive (*ibtidāʾī*) *jihād*: This is for the sake of spreading Islam and breaking down the barriers that tyrants erect in the face of Islam and guidance. In this case, the Muslims and their legitimate leadership may initiate the fighting if tyrants were standing in the way of propagating guidance among the people. In the jurists' opinion, this type of fighting is limited to a certain category of people comprising healthy, strong men. It does not include all men, for those who are too weak to fight – as mentioned in the Noble Qur'ān: the sick, the lame, the blind, the elderly, or other people who are characterized with other such features that indicate weakness – have permission to forego *jihād*. Allah ﷻ has said: "There is no blame on the weak, nor on the sick, nor on those who do not find anything to spend, so long as they are sincere to Allah and His Apostle. There is no [cause for] blaming the virtuous, and Allah is all-forgiving, all-merciful."[4]

2- Defensive *jihād*: This is if the tyrants and the faithless attacked the Muslims and aggressed against them. In this case, the Muslims must defend the religion and realm of Islam and the Muslims as per a reliable

[4] Sūrat al-Tawba, verse 91.

ḥadīth related from Ahl al-Bayt ﷺ[5], without regard to bodily strength or weakness.

In such a case, *jihād* would be incumbent on anyone who is capable of it, regardless if they are men or women, and whether they are bodily sound or infirm, such as the blind and the lame and others. *Jihād* here is a defensive obligation that is incumbent on everyone who could defend Islam or contribute to the defensive operation.

Doubtlessly, the battle of Imām al-Ḥusayn ؑ classifies as defensive *jihād*; Imām al-Ḥusayn ؑ engaged in *jihād* and defended Islam when it was being endangered by the rule of the tyrannical ruler Yazīd who was attempting to lead the Muslims away from Islam and propound misguided concepts that are antithetical to Islam.

The ruling permitting *jihād* in such a case is not unique to Yazīd. Rather, it extends to all tyrants who have Yazīd-like qualities, so to

[5] From Yunus, from Abū al-Ḥasan al-Riḍā ؑ that he said, "He [the weak person] should mobilize at the front without fighting. If the situation escalates to an extent causing him to fear for the realm of Islam and Muslims, he should fight."

speak. In such a case, *jihād* would be defensive, encompassing and including all those who are capable, regardless of the nature of their capability. For this reason, it encompasses women as well.

Secondly, women's *jihād* in the uprising of Karbalā' was not actually obligatory, which is why not all the women participated in it. This was for many reasons, explained below.

An immense benefit had to do with the second phase of Imām al-Ḥusayn's ﷺ battle. It is the phase when the women were left to perform the other roles that I will mention later. This is why Imām al-Ḥusayn ﷺ forbade some women from getting actively involved in the fighting. Despite this, it's noteworthy that women's involvement in the fighting was not non-existent.

There are examples of women who were so involved, such as:

1- Umm Wahab bt. ʿAbdullāh, who was at Karbalā' with her husband ʿAbdullāh b. ʿUmayr al-Kalbī, of the ʿAlīm clan and whose teknonym was Abū Wahab. When Umm Wahab's husband went to fight, killing Yasār the bondsman of Ziyād and Sālim the bondsman of ʿUbayd Allah b. Ziyād, he came back to Imām al-Ḥusayn ﷷ and waxed poetic in the *rajaz* meter about his heroic acts. His wife Umm Wahab went to him carrying a tentpole and said, "May my father and mother ransom you. Defend the good, the progeny of Muḥammad ﷺ." He wanted to return her to the tent, but she refused. She clutched at his garments and said, "I will not leave you except that I die with you." Imām al-Ḥusayn ﷷ called out to her, "Allah reward you both with goodness on behalf of your Prophet's household. Go back, for fighting is not incumbent on women." At this, she went back, but after her husband was captured and then killed, she walked out to him and sat at his head, cleaning the blood off it and saying, "Congratulations on attaining Paradise. I ask Allah who granted you Paradise to take me to you." At this, al-Shimr said to his servant Rustum, "Hit her in the head with the pole." Rustum gave her a head wound and she died immediately. She was the first woman among the companions of Imām al-Ḥusayn ﷺ to be killed.[6]

2- Umm ʿAbdullāh b. ʿUmayr al-Kalbī: After her son was killed, they cut off his head and threw it back to Imām al-Ḥusayn's ﷺ side. She took her son's head and wiped the blood off it, then she picked up a tentpole and stood before the enemy. Imām al-Ḥusayn ﷺ stopped her and said to her, "Allah have mercy on you, go back, for *jihād* is not a duty upon you."[7]

3- Umm ʿAmr b. Junāda al-Anṣārī: Her son was eleven years old. He came and asked Imām al-Ḥusayn ﷺ for permission to fight, but the Imām was averse to allow him, saying, "This is a boy whose father was killed in the first operation. Perhaps his mother dislikes his participation." However, the boy replied, "My mother herself commanded me to seek your permission," so the Imām ﷺ allowed him to fight. Soon after the boy was killed, and his head was thrown beside Imām al-Ḥusayn's ﷺ, the mother of the boy took

[6] Al-Muqarram, *Maqtal al-Ḥusayn* ﷺ, 238, 242.

[7] Ibid.

her son's head, wiped off the blood, and used it as a weapon to kill one of the enemies nearby. She went back to the campsite and picked up a tentpole, and Imām al-Ḥusayn عليه السلام returned her to the tent after she struck two men with the pole.[8]

4- Tawʿa: She gave shelter to Muslim b. ʿAqīl and hid him in her house in Kūfa when ʿUbayd Allah b. Ziyād went after him. This good woman took it upon herself to protect Muslim b. ʿAqīl and subjected herself, her very being, and her home to the extreme dangers of combat.

There are also other positions displayed by the wives of the Imāms' عليهم السلام enemies, expressing their objection to this monstrous crime. In this regard, there is the position of al-Nawwār, wife of Kaʿb b. Jābir, who participated in the killing of Burayr b. Khuḍayr. She held it against her husband and said, "You have aided in the killing of the son of Fāṭima عليها السلام. You killed the master of the reciters of the Qur'ān, and committed a horrible deed. By Allah, I will never speak to

[8] Ibid., 253.

you of my own volition again."[9] Such is the position of dissociation (*al-barāʾa*) from the Enemies of Allah ﷻ, and it complements the position of association (*wilāya*) and fidelity to the Friends of Allah. Indeed, there are many such honorable examples.

[9] Ibid., 250.

Preserving the Virtuous Remnant (al-Baqiyya al-Ṣāliḥa)[10]

The second role is safeguarding the virtuous remnant of the Household of Prophethood ﷺ and their supporters and followers. In Islamic human history in general, and in the Ḥusaynī uprising in particular, women have had a great role in safeguarding the virtuous remnant. Imām ʿAlī ؑ speaks of the importance of this remnant in a well-known saying of his: "The remnant of the sword is more prosperous." This means that those who survive the sword are more prosperous and have a greater influence on the outcomes of the battle. When a person engages in a battle and fights with his sword, this sword may break with nothing but a shard of it remaining. Of course, this is a metaphorical expression, as the sword at times signifies this mere blade of iron that's used in combat, and at other times signifies the moral (*maʿnawī*) aspect, namely the might in

[10] What is meant by this expression is that what remained of the legacy of virtue after the struggle of the Prophet ﷺ and his holy progeny, especially after the uprising of Imām al-Ḥusayn ؑ, was preserved by women.

fighting the enemies and attaining the upper hand on the way to victory. The sword also signifies the warriors who engage in the fighting. The Imām ﷺ refers to these warriors metaphorically by saying that those who are left after the sword and the military battle are more prosperous, pure, and more capable of fulfilling perfection in future Islamic and *jihādi* movements.

Therefore, preserving this last remnant that survives the sword is an important aspect of carrying on with the uprising and revolution, as this remnant has an important role in the spheres of politics and *jihād.*

Here we notice an equality at the level of human and Islamic history generally – encompassing all the divine religions that Allah ﷻ sent down, as "religion is submission to Allah"[11] – and the particular history of the revolt of Imām al-Ḥusayn ﷺ.

We notice that women have had a great role in this regard. The Noble Qur'ān itself

[11] Sūrat Āl 'Imrān, verse 19.

mentions a number of examples, as does Islamic history more generally.

For instance, the primary role in safeguarding Prophet Ibrāhīm عليه السلام fell to his mother, as some religious texts relate. His uncle had wanted to kill him because of a dream that Namrūd had, but his mother interceded with his uncle, who apparently was a custodian of her affairs and life, and she was able to safeguard Ibrāhīm عليه السلام. A *ḥadīth* related from Imām al-Ṣādiq عليه السلام states that "when the mother of Ibrāhīm brought Ibrāhīm into her home, Āzar looked at her inquiringly. Ibrāhīm's mother then said to him, 'Don't worry. For if the king doesn't know that he is here, we get to keep our son."[12]

Furthermore, history relates the role of Hājar عليها السلام which was essential in safeguarding Ismāʿīl عليه السلام who is the extension of Ibrāhīm عليه السلام. The extension of Ibrāhīm عليه السلام in Islamic and religious history finds expression in the path of Ismāʿīl and Isḥāq عليهما السلام, and the path of

[12] *Al-Biḥār*, 12: 29-34, chapter on the birth of Ibrāhīm عليه السلام.

Ismāʿīl ﷺ is the path of our Prophet Muḥammad ﷺ.[13]

The next historical example is that of Mūsā ﷺ. The Noble Qur'ān emphasizes the role of Firʿawn's wife in safeguarding him at a time when Pharaoh wanted to kill him: "Firʿawn's wife said [to Firʿawn], '[This infant will be] a [source of] comfort to me and to you. Do not kill him. Maybe he will benefit us, or we will adopt him as a son.'"[14]

The Noble Qur'ān also told us about the role of Maryam ﷺ in caring for ʿĪsā ﷺ, and spoke of her as exemplary in safeguarding him. She endured immense emotional pressure due to the mysterious and unusual birth of ʿĪsā ﷺ: "Then carrying him she brought him to her

---

[13] The Qur'ān highlights this in the supplication of Ibrāhīm and Ismāʿīl ﷺ when they raised the foundations of the House by referring to the submissive progeny that would encompass the Prophet ﷺ: "As Ibrāhīm raised the foundations of the House with Ismāʿīl, [they prayed]: 'Our Lord, accept it from us! Indeed You are the All-hearing, the All-knowing. 'Our Lord, make us submissive to You, and [raise] from our progeny a nation submissive to You, and show us our rites [of worship], and turn to us clemently. Indeed You are the All-clement, the All-merciful. 'Our Lord, raise amongst them an apostle from among them, who should recite to them Your signs, and teach them the Book and wisdom and purify them. Indeed You are the All-mighty, the All-wise.'"

[14] Sūrat al-Qaṣaṣ, verse 9.

people. They said, 'O Maryam, you have certainly come up with an odd thing! O sister of Hārūn['s lineage]! Your father was not an evil man, nor was your mother unchaste.'"[15]

When we get to the history of early Islam as represented in the Muḥammad an message, women have also had a role, as represented by Khadīja ؑ who stood by the Prophet of Allah ؐ financially and supported him by her own faith and through her defense of him, so much that the Prophet mentioned her in a *ḥadīth*: "She has a house in Paradise made of gemstones, pearls encrusted with gold, free of fatigue and uproar."[16] Such was her importance and her role that the well-known saying goes: "Islam was built upon Khadīja's money and ʿAlī's sword."

Sayyida Fāṭima al-Zahrā ؑ also had such a role after the death of the Prophet ؐ when she was able to safeguard Imām ʿAlī ؑ after he refused to pledge allegiance and his life was endangered, in addition to safeguarding the principle of *wilaya* and belief in ʿAlī ؑ.

---

[15] Sūrat Maryam, verses 27-28.

[16] *Al-Biḥār*, 16:20-76, and 18: 241-243.

History relates to us examples of women's roles in safeguarding the last remnant who may suffer grave dangers as they engage in *jihād* and uprising.

Sayyida Zaynab ﷺ was able to undertake an extraordinary role in the revolution of Imām al-Ḥusayn ﷺ by safeguarding the life of Imām Zayn al-'Ābidīn ﷺ, who was the remnant of prophethood and the house of revelation and divine message, and an extension of the Imāmate. She is well-known for her responses in two situations:[17]

The first situation was when Imām al-Ḥusayn ﷺ was killed and the army of ʿUmar b. Saʿd monstrously attacked the campsite of the Imām. They made their way to ʿAlī b. al-Ḥusayn ﷺ who was in his sickbed, too ill to stand. Some of them cried out, "Do not leave anyone alive, neither young nor old." While others said, "Wait and don't be hasty about this. Let us consult our commander, ʿUmar b. Saʿd." Suddenly, al-Shimr unsheathed his sword, intending to kill ʿAlī b. al-Ḥusayn ﷺ.

[17] The existence of other situations that were not written down and recorded is historically plausible because not all the details and events of Karbalāʾ have been recorded.

ʿUmar b. Saʿd stopped him, particularly after he heard Sayyida Zaynab ﷺ say, "death shall not touch him unless it touches me first."[18]

The second situation was in the court of ʿUbayd Allah b. Ziyād. History tells us that when the captives were brought into the presence of ʿUbayd Allah b. Ziyād in Kūfā, he saw among the women one man, i.e. ʿAlī b. al-Ḥusayn al-Sajjād ﷺ. ʿUbayd Allah b. Ziyād found it odd, so he turned to him and asked, "What's your name?" The Imām replied, "I am ʿAlī b. al-Ḥusayn." Ibn Ziyād wondered, "Didn't Allah kill ʿAlī b. al-Ḥusayn?" so al-Sajjād ﷺ said, "An elder brother of mine was called ʿAlī, and the people killed him." Ibn Ziyād was undeterred: "It was Allah indeed who killed him." At this, al-Sajjād ﷺ recited: "Allah takes the souls at the time of their death,"[19] "No soul may die except by Allah's leave."[20] Ibn Ziyād became indignant and ordered that ʿAlī b. al-Ḥusayn ﷺ be put to the sword, whereupon his aunt Sayyida

[18] Al-Muqarram, *Maqtal al-Ḥusayn* ﷺ, 301.

[19] Sūrat al-Zumar, verse 42.

[20] Sūrat Āl ʿImrān, verse 145.

Zaynab 🕊 hugged him and said to Ibn Ziyād, "Our blood that you've already shed should be enough for you, O Ibn Ziyād! Indeed, did you leave anyone except him?! If you are intent on killing him, you have to kill me with him." Al-Sajjād 🕊 said, "Don't you know that we are no strangers to being killed, and that Allah bestows His bounty on us through martyrdom?" Ibn Ziyād looked at the two of them and said, "Let her have him. How wondrous are blood relations; she longed to be killed with him!"[21]

There are other situations when Sayyida Zaynab 🕊 safeguarded the last remnant of the offspring of the Prophet of Allah 🕊 and the Ahl al-Bayt 🕊. The day of ʿĀshūrā hardly left alive any man of the Ahl al-Bayt 🕊, except those of them who were unable to engage in battle or those who stayed back in Medina such as ʿAbdullāh b. Jaʿfar and Muḥammad b. al-Ḥanafiyya who were unable to participate. Only the children were left. Had Sayyida Zaynab 🕊 been unable to safeguard them, the Ahl al-Bayt 🕊 would have been eradicated.

---

[21] Al-Muqarram, *Maqtal al-Ḥusayn* 🕊, 325.

Here the Commander of the Faithful's ﷺ saying about the remnant of the sword comes to mind again. Were one able to observe the Ahl al-Bayt ﷺ on the day of ʿAshūrā on the 61st year of the Hijra, one would imagine that they had gone out of existence, without a trace. This is because the rallying cry of Ibn Saʿd and his men had been: "Keep no one belonging to this household alive."[22]

Despite that, the remnant of the sword has prospered, thrived, and spread to every corner of the earth, raising the banner of Islam in all ages and times.

In our day and age, this last remnant is bearing the banner of Islam, as represented by Imām Khomeini ؒ and the other scholars and *marājiʿ* (may Allah have mercy on those who have passed and safeguard the living).

There are other stances in history taken by faithful women during the battle of Karbalāʾ. History relates that when a woman of the Bakr b. Wāʾil clan witnessed the burning of

---

[22] This is similar to the announcement of the criminal Ṣaddām after the revolt of 15 Shaʿban, 1411 AH when he stated that the Shiites were no more in Iraq.

the Imām's campsite and the brutal attack on the household of prophethood, she came out of ʿUmar b. Saʿd's camp and shouted, "O Bakr b. Wāʾil, is it right for the daughters of the Prophet of Allah ﷺ to suffer plunder? Judgment belongs to Allah. Vengeance for the Apostle of Allah!"[23]

Such stances put the Umayyad army in a precarious position comprised by the state of emotional shifts and the torrents of feeling that could have ignited the psychological and political situation in favor of the Ahl al-Bayt ﷺ, reversing the fortunes of ʿUmar b. Saʿd. This made Ibn Saʿd act quickly and forbid the killing of anyone, after which he put a stop to the pillaging and plundering.

By considering these historical incidents, we understand the significance of the special role that women could have.

I ask my dear brothers the researchers and preachers who discuss such topics and dimensions to keep using such terms so that they be an example and a lesson to us in

[23] Al-Muqarram, *Maqtal al-Ḥusayn* ﷺ, 301.

these times, and a lesson to our honorable sisters and women on how contributing to Imām al-Ḥusayn's ﷺ revolution can happen at any day and age. The revolution of Imām al-Ḥusayn ﷺ is not a revolution for a handful of days, limited to the year 61 AH. It is a revolution that continues and remains as far as we're concerned, for every day is ʿAshūrā and every land is Karbalāʾ.

Preserving Values and Morals

The third role is preserving the values, ideals, and morals that Imām al-Ḥusayn عليه السلام rose to uphold and defend in his revolt and blessed uprising.

The revolution of Imām al-Ḥusayn عليه السلام has a number of important dimensions that I briefly touched upon in my book about the revolution of Imām al-Ḥusayn عليه السلام. Of these important primary dimensions is the moral dimension of the revolution. In his own time, Imām al-Ḥusayn عليه السلام was facing a collapse of morality within Muslim society. This nascent society, this nation that was the best nation ever brought forth for mankind, was able to achieve great things and spread guidance and righteousness all over the world, and it expanded greatly in the formative era of Islam. It spread throughout the East and West by way of vast conquests, both East toward Persia and West toward Byzantium. Indeed, Islam expanded exponentially in the formative years of Islam.

Ethics are an important aspect of Islamic theory. They are the bedrock of Muslim society in Islamic theory. In Islamic theory, society is strong and capable of surviving and subsisting if it stands on two foundations.

The first foundation is creed (*'aqīda)*: In Islam, creed is represented by the belief in monotheism, and all of its branches—from Prophethood, extending to Imāmate, and the belief in the Hereafter and Punishment and Reward; whose extension is believing in Allah's ﷻ justice. Creed is the most important foundation for the stability of any society. If the creed is solid, sound, authentic, and clear, society will be stable and strong. In contrast, if this creed is flimsy, false, erroneous, and ambiguous, society will be shaky, weak, liable to the impulses of desire and endangered by any accident.

This is why creed is so important. In the first period of its revelation, during the Meccan Period, the Noble Qur'ān primarily focused on creed for the purpose of establishing this important foundation in Muslim society.

The second foundation is morality (*akhlāq*), expressed by values and ideals within human life. Morality entails a special understanding of man's character and his nature of seeking perfection, given to him by Allah ﷻ, and expressed as his primordial nature (*fiṭra*), and his perception of the goodness (*ḥusn*) and perfection of justice compared to injustice. Likewise, man also perceives the truth of freedom compared to the fetters and servitude of desire, fear, superstition, and illusion. He understands the components of his own perfection such as promise-keeping, patience in hardships, and firmness on the (righteous) path. On the other hand are the components of his downfall and degradation, such as treachery, fickleness, despair, and abandoning just causes (*khidhlān*). There are many other values that Islam stresses using a variety of terms.

As an example, being truthful is one of these values, as is keeping one's promises, and being patient.

So is trustworthiness (*amāna*) and holding oneself accountable to Allah ﷻ, society, and one's obligations. Both values are important values that the Qur'an emphasized: "Indeed We presented the Trust to the heavens and the earth and the mountains, but they refused to bear it, and were apprehensive of it; but man undertook it. Indeed he is most unfair and senseless."[24]

These morals, values, and ideals are the second solid foundation, next to creed, upon which the Muslim society stands.

In the era of Imām al-Ḥusayn, people's morals suffered a blow due to the indulgence in worldliness, the intransigence of desires and pleasures, the abundance of money, and the growth of power and authority, in addition to other things that led to the weakening of morality.

This is why when it comes to Imām al-Ḥusayn, we notice two opposing trends of behavior. The first was the Imām's enemies' behavior toward him, which was utterly low and morally bankrupt. As for the second kind of behavior, it was the Imām's behavior

---

[24] Sūrat al-Aḥzāb, verse 72.

toward his enemies, which was always morally upstanding and noble at the level of feelings, emotions, and deeds.

When we reflect on the biography of Imām al-Ḥusayn عليه السلام and his uprising, from the moment he set out from Medina until his martyrdom, we notice these two trends, the one represented by Imām al-Ḥusayn's عليه السلام enemies and the other represented by him and his companions. The moral issue was one of the key issues of the battle.

Imām al-Ḥusayn عليه السلام wanted to stir up the conscience and feeling of these people, referred to in Islam as the primordial nature according to which Allah عز وجل originated mankind. As for the philosophers and theologians, they refer to this primordial nature and its objects of cognition as practical reason (*al-ʿaql al-ʿamalī*), whereas the Noble Qur'ān refers to it as the sentient heart that knows things and that may die or become diseased or sealed. The heart is the perceiving side of us, namely behavioral perception, and it is sometimes referred to as rational morality (*al-ḥusn wal-qubḥ al-aqliyyayn*).

Allah ﷻ made the perceptions of practical reason part of man's nature, allowing him to perceive goodness and badness. That's why when a person examines certain behaviors according to his primordial nature, he is able to distinguish the good from the bad. For instance, a person perceives, and apprehends using his mind, that trustworthiness is a good thing, even if he is not personally trustworthy. In the same way, a person knows treachery is a bad thing even if he is actually treacherous. The same thing happens when it comes to truthfulness and lying, or patience and steadfastness and constancy versus fickleness and cowardice and despair.

Through his practical reason, and through the objects of perception of his primordial nature, given him by Allah ﷻ, man perceives that such a thing is good and such a thing is bad, regardless of his own behavior. When he persistently does not commit to good behavior, his primordial nature undergoes deviation and becomes an unwavering foundation that causes him to behave in a degraded and low manner. A society in which such behavior is prevalent falls apart at the moral level, which was what happened in the era of Imām al-Ḥusayn عليه السلام.

Imām al-Ḥusayn عليه السلام revolted to safeguard values, and he made sacrifices for the sake of the public good, for Islam, and for people as a whole, as he said, "I did not revolt out of pride or arrogance nor out of a desire to cause corruption or commit tyranny. I only revolted seeking reform in the nation of my grandfather. I seek to enjoin good and forbid evil, command the right and forbid the wrong, and walk in the footsteps of my grandfather and my father ʿAlī b. Abī Ṭālib."[25]

After Imām al-Ḥusayn عليه السلام was martyred, the path of morality had to continue and reach its perfection.

Women had a major role in safeguarding these values. Let us assume that Imām al-Ḥusayn's عليه السلام womenfolk did not commit to a

[25] *Al-Biḥār*, 44, 329.

certain moral standard—Allah forbid—what would have happened to the movement of Imām al-Ḥusayn ﷺ at the moral level?

This is perfectly clear in Sayyida Zaynab ﷺ, the good woman and the good exemplar, and her stances. She rose up in the court of Ibn Ziyād, who took himself to be victorious, and he was giddy with victory. Keeping in mind that he was a bad person and an impetuous youth, he tried to express his impetuousness by expressing schadenfreude toward Sayyida Zaynab ﷺ and Imām al-Ḥusayn ﷺ. This is why he asked Sayyida Zaynab ﷺ, "How do you like what Allah did to that brother of yours and to your people?" Here, Sayyida Zaynab ﷺ showed faith in Allah ﷻ and patience during calamity, as well as a keen understanding of this revolution's goals, for she responded, "I saw nothing but beauty. They were people whom Allah destined to be slain and they set out toward the places where they were laid to rest. Allah will bring you together with them and they will argue and dispute with you. Wait and see who will be victorious on that day. May your mother be bereft of you, O son of Marjāna."[26]

This faithful group of people fulfilled its responsibility to the utmost, bore this matter, and put up with harm for the sake of the public good and for the sake of pleasing Allah ﷻ and attaining these levels of perfection.

If we reflect on her sermon in Kūfa (Iraq), we find that this sermon aimed to admonish the people and emphasize the morals that they should have had, referencing their treachery, abandonment of the Imām, and the breaking of their covenants and going back on their word: "Do you cry and weep? Yes indeed, cry much and laugh but little. You have borne the shame and hatred (or disgrace) of your deed, and you will not wash it off of you for as long as you live. You committed a grievous, horrible, heinous thing indeed."[27]

Likewise is her sermon in Yazīd's court which was teeming with notables, leaders,

[26] Ibid., 45: 115-116.

[27] Ibid., 45: 109.

viziers, princes, and ambassadors. Yazīd brought them together from everywhere near and far to gloat about his victory. And yet, Sayyida Zaynab ﷺ stood resolute and spoke to Yazīd sternly, "Is it fair, you son of freed-captives, that you cover up your women, both free and slave women, while you take the daughters of the Prophet of Allah ﷺ as captives? You violated their covers and put their faces on display, making their enemies drive them from place to place while travelers look at them and those near and far and lowly and noble stare at their faces. Not one of their menfolk or protectors is with them. And yet, how might we hope for discretion from those whose mouths spit out the livers of the pure and whose flesh grew on the blood of martyrs? I swear to you: you only cut up your own skin and you only chopped up your own flesh."[28]

There are other stances displayed by women who are not at Sayyida Zaynab's ﷺ level of virtue and knowledge. They were seemingly ordinary women, but in their moral behavior, they were lofty, great, and struggling women.

[28] Ibid., 45: 133-135.

An example is Dalham (or Daylam), the wife of Zuhayr b. al-Qayn, who used to be *Uthmanid.* This means that he used to believe that ʿUthmān was unjustly killed and that he must be avenged. Like Muʿāwiya, he accused ʿAlī's ﷺ companions of killing ʿUthmān, which is why he was trying to avoid meeting Imām al-Ḥusayn ﷺ on the way, always opting to dismount elsewhere. At some point, however, he was forced to dismount at the same place because it had water, and Zuhayr's party needed water. Imām al-Ḥusayn ﷺ took advantage of this opportunity to convince Zuhayr to join him as he saw himself responsible and called to him anyone who might be fit for such an undertaking.

Shaykh al-Majlisī relates from *Kitāb al-Malhūf*, from some people from the clans of Fazāra and Bujayla that they said, "We were with Zuhayr b. al-Qayn of the clan of Bujayla on our way from Mecca, and we traveled the same paths as Imām al-Ḥusayn ﷺ. There was nothing that we detested more than dismounting in the same place as Imām al-Ḥusayn ﷺ. If Imām al-Ḥusayn ﷺ dismounted at a certain place and we absolutely had to dismount at that same place, we took to dismounting some distance away from Imām al-Ḥusayn عليه السلام. While we were sitting for our midday meal, Imām al-Ḥusayn's عليه السلام messenger came and saluted us then entered our tent. He said, 'O Zuhayr b. al-Qayn, Abā ʿAbdillāh sends for you.' Everyone dropped the food that they had in hand out of shock and sat motionless. Zuhayr's wife, Daylam bt. ʿAmr said to him, "What a strange thing! Can it be that the son of the Prophet of Allah is sending for you and you do not go?"[29]

This good woman did not even know the particulars of the invitation. Simply the prospect of her husband refusing the invitation of Imām al-Ḥusayn عليه السلام, son of the Prophet of Allah ﷺ, was antithetical to good morals in her view. This is why she took it upon herself to urge her husband to accept the invitation and go meet the Imām عليه السلام. The fruit of that meeting was that Zuhayr underwent a 180-degree change—as the expression goes from an opposing Uthmanid to an advocate and a supporter who was

[29] Ibid., 44: 371.

ready to sacrifice everything in the way of Imām al-Ḥusayn ﷺ and his path.

The reason for that was that Imām al-Ḥusayn ﷺ reminded Zuhayr of a conversation that the latter had with Salmān al-Fārisī during the war to liberate Iraq when Allah ﷻ made them victorious and they won many spoils. Salman said to the people, "Are you happy with Allah's victory and the spoils that you won?" They said, "Yes." He said, "If you live to the time of the master of the youth of Muḥammad 's household, let your happiness about fighting on his side be greater than your happiness in these spoils."[30] At this, Zuhayr remembered the incident and joined Imām al-Ḥusayn ﷺ.

Another woman who took a moral stance was al-Nawwar (who we mentioned earlier) when she spoke to her husband Kaʿb b. Jabir about Burayr, the master of the reciters of the Noble Qur'ān. Kaʿb should have observed Burayr's rights as an educator. Instead, he was unfaithful to Burayr despite the latter's many services to society. Al-Nawwar said to

[30] Al-Muqarram, *Maqtal al-Ḥusayn* ﷺ, 177 from *Tārīkh al-Ṭabarī*.

her husband, "You have aided in the killing of the son of Fāṭima ﷺ. You killed the master of the reciters of the Qur'ān, and committed a horrible deed. By Allah, I will never speak to you of my own volition again."[31] This is just one of many noble stances that aimed to safeguard morality.

This is why we stress the immense responsibility of the families, wives, mothers, and sisters of martyrs, and the responsibility of anyone belonging to these esteemed families to safeguard the moral position that the martyrs laid down their lives for, and to which they had the honor of belonging to.

---

[31] Ibid., 250.

The Role of Publicity

The fourth role of women, and particularly Sayyida Zaynab عليها السلام, was the role of publicity, for which she bore the primary responsibility.

In this regard, we should first point out the importance of publicity in the realm of politics and *jihād*. Secondly, we should speak of the methodology and goals of this publicity. Afterward, we will speak of the role of faithful women, and particularly Sayyida Zaynab عليها السلام, in the uprising of the Imām عليه السلام.

The Importance of Publicity in Politics

First, in any political and *jihādi* movement, publicity is of utmost importance. These two domains cannot be productive and effective without publicity. If we go back to the roots of publicity, it seems that its essence derives from the promulgation (*al-Balagh)* that is undertaken by prophets and messengers, for the primary responsibility of any prophet is to promulgate the message. This promulgation sometimes encapsulates all the dimensions of a prophet's duty: "The

Messenger's duty is only to deliver 'the message'..."[32] From this verse, it seems that sometimes promulgation is a prophet's sole responsibility.

Sometimes this duty is the first in a series of responsibilities undertaken by the prophets and messengers, as mentioned in the verse: "It is He who sent to the unlettered [people] an apostle from among themselves, to recite to them His signs, to purify them, and to teach them the Book and wisdom, and earlier they had indeed been in manifest error."[33]

In this verse, a messenger has three main responsibilities: to recite the (holy verses, to purify the people, to educate them, and to teach them the Book and Wisdom (*al-kitāba wal-ḥikma*). The promulgation expressed in this holy verse as "reciting the signs" is at the forefront of these responsibilities, for publicity is the main and primary role in the transformative mission of prophets and messengers.

---

[32] Sūrat al-Mā'ida, verse 99.

[33] Sūrat al-Jumu'a, verse 2.

Allah described his prophets who fully commit to their missions and promulgate the obligations and duties that He assigned them, with the following: "such as deliver the messages of Allah and fear Him, and fear no one except Allah, and Allah suffices as the reckoner."[34]

Publicizing the Ḥusaynī Uprising

The main reason for the Ḥusaynī uprising's continuation and success was the special role of the last remnant of the Ahl al-Bayt in speaking out and clarifying the uprising's circumstances and goals, and communicating its message to the people.

This role was first undertaken by Imām Zayn al-ʿĀbidīn, being the last remnant of the Ahl al-Bayt, and second by Sayyida Zaynab and the rest of the Ahl al-Bayt.

Obviously, the success of publicity requires a proper methodology and style by keeping in mind the circumstances, mentalities, and emotional statuses of the audience, as well as

[34] Sūrat al-Aḥzāb, 39.

the important causes to which the nation (*umma*) responds.

This is eloquence (*balāgha*), which linguists define as "the conformity of the utterance to the requirements of the situation (*muṭābaqat al-kalām li-muqtaḍā al-ḥāl*)." It is different from fluency (*faṣāḥa*), as fluency refers to when speech is correct and in conformity with the rules of a given language, and when the choice of words is accurate, excellent, and effective.

Eloquence requires the conformity of speech to people's lived experience so that political rhetoric would have an effect on them.

While other women had certain lesser roles in publicity, Sayyida Zaynab had the greatest role. When she decided to undertake the mission of publicizing the Imām's cause, being the symbol of all women involved in this uprising, Sayyida Zaynab's promulgation and political rhetoric had four stages. In all four of these stages, she chose the words of her promulgation and political rhetoric carefully to suit the circumstances.

Stage one was publicity in the days before or shortly after the beginning of the battle. She spoke on the eve and on the day of ʿAshūrā, i.e. the day the Imām عليه السلام was martyred, while the battle was raging, on the eve of the eleventh day, and on the eleventh day when the march to Kūfa began. She mainly focused on stirring the enemies' feelings and emotions.

We notice this when she went to Imām al-Ḥusayn عليه السلام after he was killed. ʿUmar b. Saʿd and some of his entourage approached Imām al-Ḥusayn عليه السلام in his final moments, so she yelled, "O ʿUmar, Is Abū ʿAbdillāh to die while you simply look on?" Ibn Saʿd then looked away, his tears drenching his beard.[35]

Her words عليها السلام moved his hard heart, and he expressed his feelings by shedding emotive tears. Afterward, she loudly called out in order to move those present: "O, Muḥammad! O, father! O, ʿAlī! Oh, Jaʿfar! O, Hamza! Here

---

[35] Al-Tabari, 4:345, al-Aʿlami's edition.

is al-Ḥusayn, lying out in the open, dead in Karbalāʾ." She then yelled, "If only the sky fell upon the earth! If only the mountains tumbled over the plains!"

On the eleventh day, when she wanted to part from Imām al-Ḥusayn ﷺ for the last time, she cried out, "O Muḥammad! Here is al-Ḥusayn, out in the open, imbued in his own blood, his organs dismembered, and your daughters are now captives," causing both friend and foe to cry.[36]

Although the main concern of this uprising was drawing closer to Allah ﷻ and having a relationship to Him, as well as upholding certain principles, Sayyida Zaynab's ﷺ speech aimed to incite the lofty emotions that Allah ﷻ built into man's primordial nature in order to move the people's consciences and transform their psychological and spiritual realities.

Even if Sayyida Zaynab ﷺ did not fully achieve this goal during the battle or in the

[36] Al-Muqarram, *Maqtal al-Ḥusayn* ﷺ, 284, 307. See also *al-Biḥār*, 45: 55, 58-59 and al-Ṭabarī, 4: 348, al-Aʿlamī's edition.

short term, this stage was the most crucial stage in transforming the spiritual and psychological reality the people were living in.

The second stage was when Sayyida Zaynab عليها السلام spoke in Kūfa, where the general political and psychological atmosphere was one of support and sympathy to the Ahl al-Bayt عليهم السلام. In addition, the Kufans had entered in covenants and pledges to fight on Imām al-Ḥusayn's عليه السلام side, and their hearts were indeed with him, but they abandoned him at the last moment for many reasons, such as the number of arrests made, the pressures and threats of the rulers, and the many temptations offered to people to buy them off.

All these factors bred a sense of defeat among the people.

When Sayyida Zaynab and Fāṭima bt. al-Ḥusayn عليهما السلام and others spoke to the Kufans, their speeches revolved around rebuking the Kufans for breaking their pledges and covenants, which moved many of them and caused them to cry bitter tears. These people regretted their actions and began mobilizing immediately as an expression of their regret. This means that Sayyida Zaynab's عليها السلام speech was an eloquent political speech that she chose to match the political and spiritual circumstances.

Stage three is the stage of Sayyida Zaynab عليها السلام speaking to the people of Shām, i.e. the Ahl al-Bayt's عليهم السلام traditional enemies, who took to gloating after Karbalāʾ. Although her previous words and speeches were also directed at enemies, the general audience at that time were sympathetic to the Ahl al-Bayt عليهم السلام; the general atmosphere in Kūfa after the killing of Imām al-Ḥusayn عليه السلام was of sadness and tears. In Shām, however, things were different. The people of Shām were antagonistic to the Ahl al-Bayt عليهم السلام. The reigning social atmosphere there was one of happiness and joy to the extent that Shām was decorated in celebration of the killing of Imām al-Ḥusayn عليه السلام.

This is why the content and style of the speeches were different in Shām, focusing on speaking the truth and showcasing the firmess, steadfastness, and persistence of the Ahl al-Bayt ﷺ and their perseverance on this path, as well as their remaining on the side of the truth and speaking of a future time when the faithful will indeed be victorious.

Stage four is the stage of post-captivity when Sayyida Zaynab ﷺ settled in Medina and then was banished to Egypt, as some narrations relate.[37] This banishment was calculated to exile her away from her place in Medina where her speeches changed and addressed Muslims as a whole, not solely supporters and followers as was the case in Kūfa, nor solely enemies as was the case in Shām. They became speeches to the general body of Muslims who yearned to know the truth of what happened in Karbalāʾ. In other words, Sayyida Zaynab ﷺ made her speeches at exactly the right time to ensure that they were useful and effective.

[37] Some sources mention that she was banished to Shām. The important thing is that she was banished to a place other than Medina.

Publicity in the Political Sphere

As mentioned earlier, the words of a speech must be well-chosen to suit the circumstances and the psychological and spiritual atmosphere. In this regard, we notice a number of key concepts that Sayyida Zaynab emphasized in her speeches.

The first concept is belonging to the Ahl al-Bayt who are the Prophet's family. This is something that Imām al-Ḥusayn also stressed in his political speeches before his enemies: "Am I not the son of the daughter of your Prophet and the son of his legatee/trustee (*waṣī*) and cousin who was the first to believe in Allah?"[38]

Both Sayyida Zaynab and Imām Zayn al-ʿĀbidīn stressed this fact, which no person can disregard, for the Noble Qur'ān itself pointed it out in a number of verses such as "Indeed Allah desires to repel all impurity from you, O People of the Household, and purify you with a thorough purification,"[39] and "Say, 'I do not ask you

---

[38] *Al-Biḥār*, 45:6.

[39] Sūrat al-Aḥzāb, verse 33.

any reward for it except love of [my] relatives,'"[40] among other verses.

Yazīd wanted to obfuscate this fact, portraying Imām al-Ḥusayn ؑ and his company as a group of *khāwarij* who rebelled and mutinied and were summarily killed. He left out their relation to the Prophet of Allah ﷺ.

Imām Zayn al-'Ābidīn ؑ made this truth known in the speech he gave in Shām: "I am the son of Mecca and Minā. I am the son of Zamzam and Ṣafā. I am the son of him who offered his garment to carry the stone of the Kaʿba. I am the son of the best man to wear garments. I am the son of the best man to walk shod and barefoot. I am the son of the best man to circumambulate the Kaʿba and walk between Ṣafā and Marwa."[41]

One might wonder: why all this talk of oneself? Is it not excessive? The answer is that the Imām ؑ wanted to inform the people of his familial ties to the Prophet ﷺ

---

[40] Sūrat al-Shūrā, verse 23.

[41] *Al-Biḥār* 45: 174, *ḥadīth* 22.

because Yazīd and the Umayyads wanted this fact covered up. This led to altering the political atmosphere even in the court of Yazīd, which made Yazīd decrease his pressure on the Ahl al-Bayt and feign regret.

The second concept is highlighting the main goals of Imām al-Ḥusayn's uprising. This uprising did not happen because of personal interests, tribal conflicts, power, material gains or other such causes that people might erroneously imagine. Rather, his uprising was for the sake of reform, enjoining good and forbidding evil, and upholding the truth. Sayyida Zaynab spoke about this in Yazīd's court: "O Allah, restore our right and exact revenge on whoever oppressed us. Make your anger fall upon the head of whoever shed our blood, violated our sanctity, killed our protectors, and stripped our coverings... You [Yazīd] left Muslims' eyes tearful and their chests heavy. Such hearts are hard, such souls tyrannical, and such bodies brimming with Allah's wrath and the Prophet's curse and teeming with Satan's spawn [...] How striking it is that pious men, the grandchildren of prophets, and the progeny of trustees are killed by the wicked hands of freed-captives and the descendants of whoredom."[42]

The third concept is the concept of injustice. Sayyida Zaynab ﷺ had a remarkable role in this regard, one that exceeded even the role of Imām Zayn al-ʿĀbidīn ﷺ. When women speak of injustice, they are more effective than men in reaching people.

Society views women as being weaker than men, and when the weak are oppressed, the injustice done to them is more moving. Transgressing against children and old people is different from transgressing against a robust young man. So too women.

This is why Sayyida Zaynab ﷺ had a great role in raising the issue of injustice, awakening consciences, and inciting feelings through the stances she took.

This happened during the Islamic Revolution in Iran as well. Women, who represent this

42 *Al-Biḥār* 45:157-160.

segment of human society, had a spectacular role in moving people.

The fourth concept relates to hope and the future and stresses that victory and the upper hand will belong to the uprising of Imām al-Ḥusayn ﷺ. Sayyida Zaynab ﷺ, stressed this fact in her speech to Yazīd, for she said, "Scheme and strive and strain to the best of your abilities, but I swear to you that you will not efface our memory or extinguish our revelation. You can never equal us, nor can you wash off the shame of your act. Your opinion is mere folly, your days are but numbered, and all your mustering will come to naught on the day the caller will call: 'Look! The curse of Allah is upon the wrongdoers."'[43]

Despite her difficult circumstances, which were nothing short of tragic, and the killing of her family members, not to mention her captivity and humiliation, Sayyida Zaynab ﷺ remained strong and powerful. She asserted that victory will always be on her family's side, and that Allah's ﷻ decree for them was

[43] *Al-Biḥār* 45:135, from *Kitāb al-Malhūf.*

nothing but good, stating that matters will end in their favor and that the future belongs to them.

In the realm of politics and *jihād*, spirit and morale are of utmost importance, and publicity can determine the final outcomes.

Captivity

The fifth role is the most important role of all, as it highlights women's real participation in this revolt. Women bore the second half of this revolt by standing up to injustice and tyranny and achieving the goals of Imām al-Ḥusayn ﷺ. The martyrdom of Imām al-Ḥusayn ﷺ in Karbalāʾ, and the tribulations, calamities, pain, death, and mutilation that he and his household and companions suffered represent a small part of the heinous crime that stirred even diseased or dead consciences. It was a crime that revealed the bitter truth of Yazīd's tyranny and deviance.

The other facet of this crime is the captivity and violations against Sayyida Zaynab ﷺ and the womenfolk of Imām al-Ḥusayn ﷺ and his companions. The captivity was horrible and blatant, and it had spiritual and social consequences. These women and children bore the second portion of pains and calamities. It may even be said that this portion equals that portion borne by Imām al-Ḥusayn ﷺ and his menfolk and companions.

The great tragedy of Karbalā' had two parts that complemented one another. The first part was the killing, mutilation, and violation of the paragons of our nation, at the forefront of whom was Imām al-Ḥusayn ﷺ, the son of the Prophet's daughter ﷺ, as well as his household and companions. The second part is the captivity, violation, and humiliation of the women who belonged to the household of the Prophet of Allah ﷺ.

We must point out a matter that is crucial for understanding the prevailing political atmosphere at the time. What we should highlight is the nation's religious and cultural understanding of Imām al-Ḥusayn's ﷺ movement. Once we do so, the magnificent role of Muslim women in the Ḥusaynī revolt will become clear. These women had a role in achieving the revolt's goal by stirring the conscience of the nation (*umma*), revealing the truth, and exposing the Umayyads and their position on Islam.

As for the political circumstances at the time, there was much doubt among the people about the legitimacy of the revolt and the obligation of standing up to injustice and tyranny as represented by Yazīd. Despite this, Yazīd's deviance was somewhat clear, which led some companions and followers to refrain from pledging allegiance to him.

This doubt is not noticeable in our present day. A long time has passed since the revolution of Imām al-Ḥusayn ﷺ, and it has had its effect on the Muslims and its circumstances were explained to them, revealing the truth of Yazīd and the Umayyads.

But if we were to go back to that era, the reign of Muʿāwiya b. Abī Sufyān spanned twenty years. It was an authoritarian reign that had a tight grip on the political, social, and cultural circumstances from the martyrdom of Imām ʿAlī ﷺ until the death of Muʿāwiya. The latter's rule over the Islamic world was authoritarian and autocratic, and he was most cunning and controlling, ever plotting to achieve his political, social, and cultural goals.

Amongst the ideas that Muʿāwiya strove to propagate was the idea that the ruler raising the banner of Islam must be obeyed, even if he were tyrannical, unjust, or transgressive of Islam, as long as he does not exhibit manifest unbelief in public. According to this idea, the ruler may definitely be advised and spoken to, but obeying him without question remained a religious obligation.

The aim behind the propagation of this idea was to validate Muʿāwiya's many transgressions and pave the way for Yazīd's reign, while justifying the actions of ʿUthmān and his entourage during his caliphate, and condemning those who rose against him in an attempt to stop the deviations and corrupt actions that some of his governors (*wulāt*) engaged in.

Many Prophetic *ḥadīths* were fabricated to this effect, stipulating the necessity of obeying the ruler even if he were tyrannical and unjust. These *ḥadīths* still abound to this day in many books that Muslims generally consider sound and acceptable. Muʿāwiya widely promoted these *ḥadīths*, and as the

Umayyad rule spread, they spread with it. Later, the Abbasids too accepted and promoted them.

Imām al-Ḥusayn ﵇ faced great difficulty in countering this widespread idea, and in an attempt to make things right, he narrated the following *ḥadīth* from his grandfather, the Prophet of Allah ﷺ: "... Whomsoever witnesses a tyrannical ruler, violating the sanctities of Allah, breaching the covenant with Allah, opposing the *sunnah* of the Prophet of Allah, and treating the servants of Allah sinfully and aggressively without bringing about a change through word or deed."[44]

However, things did not change, and the Imām ﵇ had difficulty in countering this view before he revolted and made sacrifices to achieve his purpose.

His battle with the Umayyads put him in a conflicting position as he was disobeying the general Islamic rulings that the Muslims

---

[44] *Al-Biḥār* 44: 382, from *al-Manāqib*. See the same *ḥadīth* with a slight difference in al-Ṭabarī 4: 304, "The Incidents of the Year 61."

were familiar with: he was revolting against the ruler who had to be obeyed. Such an act was tantamount to sowing division among the Muslims, and it was commonly lawful to kill whoever did it.

For this reason, some people have had the gall to say that Imām al-Ḥusayn ﷺ was killed with his grandfather's ﷺ sword!

In standing up to the Umayyads and revolting against them, Imām al-Ḥusayn ﷺ divulged the bitter truth of their unbelief and irreverence for Islam and its rulings. He exposed them after they committed acts that plainly violated Islam, such as the following.

The first thing they did was torture and persecute Imām al-Ḥusayn ﷺ, his household, companions, family, and children by besieging them and blocking their access to water and food. Torture is forbidden in Islam, something about which Muslims unanimously agree.

If the Umayyads were entitled to kill Imām al-Ḥusayn ﷺ, as they claimed, what was the fault of the little ones who were deprived of water and food and who died of thirst? When Imām al-Ḥusayn ﷺ was bidding his infant son ʿAbdullāh farewell, he said to him, "Woe to these people on the day when your grandfather al-Muṣṭafā will be their opponent." The Imām ﷺ carried him to the enemy camp to get water for him, but Ḥarmala b. Kāhil of the Asad clan shot him with an arrow and slew him. About the infant ʿAbdullāh al-Ḥujja ﷺ says, "Peace be upon ʿAbdullāh the infant who was shot, drowning in his blood, on his way to heaven, slain with an arrow while in his father's lap."[45]

Such a thing is plainly unacceptable. Torturing the Prophet of Allah's ﷺ household ﷺ in this monstrous manner was blatantly against Islam in the eyes of all Muslims, and no *ḥadīth* could explain or justify it.

The second thing that flagrantly went against the *Sharia* and that Imām al-Ḥusayn ﷺ was able to highlight, through his uprising and his great calamity, is mutilation. Imām

45 Al-Muqarram, *Maqtal al-Ḥusayn* ﷺ, 272.

ʿAlī ﷺ narrates that he heard the Prophet ﷺ say, "Don't you mutilate any creature, even if it be a vicious dog."[46]

Muslims of all affiliations narrate from the Prophet ﷺ that he forbade mutilation.[47]

In contrast, on the day of ʿAshūrā, ʿUmar b. Saʿd ordered his cavalry to trample on the chest and body of Imām al-Ḥusayn ﷺ in a sickening manner, and then they decapitated the dead of the Ahl al-Bayt ﷺ and the companions[48] and raised their heads on spears.

This is a kind of mutilation whose purpose is revenge and retribution, revealing the depth of the grudge that the Umayyads held and

---

46 *Al-Biḥār*, 42:246, from *Kashf al-ghumma*. See also *Nahj al-balāgha* 17:6, n. 47, from the bequest (*waṣiyya*) of Imām ʿAlī ﷺ to Imām al-Ḥasan and Imām al-Ḥusayn ﷺ after he was struck by Ibn Muljam (Allah curse him), Manshūrāt al-Marʿashī al-Najafī.

47 See *Sahīh Muslim*, 5:1357, and *Sunan Ibn Mājah*, 2: 1063. See also *Lisān al-arab*, s.v. *m.th.l.* In *Kitāb al-fiqh al Islāmi*, 6: 720 we find the following: "Mutilating anyone is forbidden whether they are alive or dead." Mutilation is defined as committing horrible acts against a dead body for the purposes of revenge and retribution.

48 See *Al-Biḥār*, 45:62, from *al-Manāqib*.

the extent of their violation of Islamic rulings.

The third act was killing the women, children, the wounded, and the debilitated for no reason other than revenge and retribution and spreading horror and fear. An example of this is the case of Umm Wahab. After her husband was captured and killed, she walked out to him and sat at his head, cleaning the blood off it. Shimr said to his servant Rustum, "Hit her in the head with the pole." Rustum gave her a head wound and she died immediately.[49]

Another example is the case of the infant ʿAbdullāh. Imām al-Ḥusayn ﷺ was bidding his infant son ʿAbdullāh farewell, and he carried him to the enemy to get water for him, but Ḥarmala b. Kāhil of the Asad clan shot him with an arrow and slew him.[50]

Some of the men in the Umayyad army, such as Shimr b. Dhī al-Jawshan, stooped so low that they even frightened the women. Others

---

49 *Al-Biḥār*, 45: 17.

50 Al-Muqarram, *Maqtal al-Ḥusayn* ﷺ, 272.

in the Umayyad camp, such as Shabath b. Ribʿī, denounced him for it. On the tenth of Muharram, "Shimr mounted an attack on the campsite of Imām al-Ḥusayn ﷺ and said, 'Give me a firebrand so that I may burn it upon the heads of those within it.' The women screamed and fled out of their tents. Shabath b. Ribʿī said to him, 'So you've taken to terrifying the women now? I have not heard a saying worse than yours nor have I witnessed an act more abominable.' Shimr felt shame and left."[51]

The fourth act, which had the greatest effect and significance in exposing the Umayyads, and which affected the public opinion of Muslim, was taking the children and women of the Prophet of Allah ﷺ captive.

There are rulings in Islamic jurisprudence concerning rebellion (*baghī*). This is a Qur'ānic term that connotes rebelling against the just ruler. In Islamic jurisprudence, killing a rebel is permissible but his household is to be kept from harm if he is a Muslim. Therefore, it is impermissible for his

[51] Ibid., 242 and al-Ṭabarī, "The Incidents of the Year 61."

family members to become captives or to be considered part of the spoils of war. This means that the women and children of rebels are treated differently from the women and children of unbelievers, whose women are taken captive, men are taken prisoner, and possessions are distributed as spoils.

The person to first make this distinction in his ruling was Imām ʿAlī ﷺ following the Battle of the Camel. Some of his men asked him to divide the spoils among them, but he categorically refused. They made their request repeatedly but he rebuked them severely, and upon their insistence, he responded with the following: "Which one of you would like to have his mother as part of the spoils?" since A'isha was the mother of the believers and was one of the captives. The men realized that he was right, for who would accept counting his own mother among the spoils? The Imām ﷺ continued by saying, "Did you not know that it is permissible to take spoils in the abode of war but that anything taken in the abode of *hijra* is impermissible unless it is taken rightfully? But wait. If you do not believe me and keep insisting so, O' good men (for many spoke up and made the same request), which one of you would like to have 'A'isha as part of his spoils?"[52] This made them understand that the legal ruling for Muslim rebels differs from the legal ruling concerning unbelievers.

It is noteworthy that Muslims of all sects and denominations abide by this legal pronouncement and accept it.[53]

In Karbalā', however, the Umayyads had a different opinion: that taking the Prophet's womenfolk and the children of Imām al-Ḥusayn and his companions captive and plundering their possessions as spoils of war is permissible!

This manifests clearly in the Umayyads holding them all captive and driving them from Karbalā' to Kūfa and then to Shām upon

---

[52] *Al-Biḥār* 32: 221-223 from al-Ṭabrisī. This was also narrated by Suyūṭī, *hadīth* 1781, from Musnad 'Alī from *Jamʿ al-Jawāmiʿ*, 2:129; al-Muttaqī al-Hindī, *Kanz al-ʿummāl*, 8:215, 1st edn., al-Tustarī, *Kitāb al-Mawāʿiẓ* from *Muntakhab kanz al-ʿummāl* with the footnotes of *Musnad Aḥmad b. Ḥanbal* 6:315, 1st edn.

[53] *al-Aḥkām al-sulṭāniyya*, 1:55, 2:58-60, on fighting the people of rebellion. See also *al-Fiqh al-Islāmī wa-adillatih*, 6:146, on fighting rebels.

emaciated she-camels, after plundering and burning their campsite. This was not enough for the Umayyads, for they chose to take their crime to still newer heights. In what follows are some examples that prove this.

First, when Abū ʿAbdillāh Imām al-Ḥusayn was killed, the enemy competed to plunder the womenfolk of the Prophet ﷺ, one snatching Umm Kulthum's earrings and wounding her ears, the other wrestling away Fāṭima bt. al-Ḥusayn's anklet as he cried. Fāṭima asked him, "O, enemy of Allah, why are you crying?" He said, "How can I not cry as I pillage the daughter of the Prophet?" She responded, "Leave me be, then," but he said, "I worry that if I don't take it, someone else will."[54]

Second, when the captives were brought into the court of Yazīd, a man from Shām saw Fāṭima bt. ʿAlī and asked Yazīd to grant her to him as a servant. Fāṭima became frightened and clung to Sayyida Zaynab and exclaimed, "Me a servant?!" Sayyida

[54] *Al-Biḥār* 45:82, *ḥadīth* 9, from *Amālī al-Ṣadūq*, 228, sitting 31, number 2 (paraphrased).

Zaynab ﵍ said, "Don't worry. That will never be!" Yazīd retorted, "If I desire it to happen, it will happen!" Sayyida Zaynab ﵍ simply said, "Then you will have apostatized."[55] Yazīd backed down in the face of this insurmountable truth.

Third, ʿAlī b. al-Ḥusayn ﵇ spent the rest of his days weeping, day and night. One of his slaves said to him, "I fear that you will perish if you continue like this." The Imām ﵇ said, "Listen. I complain of my anguish and grief only to Allah. I know from Allah what you do not know. Jacob was a prophet of whose twelve sons Allah absented one, and he went blind with grief although he knew his son was still alive. As for me, I witnessed my father, brothers, uncles, and companions dead all around me, so how can my sadness ever cease? Never do I remember the death of the sons of Fāṭima ﵍ except that I choke with tears. When I look upon my aunts and

[55] See *Amālī al-Ṣadūq*, 230, sitting 31, number 4. Al-Khawārizmī in his *Maqtal*, 2:62 stated that this incident happened with Fāṭima bt. al-Ḥusayn instead.

sisters, I recall how they were fleeing from tent to tent..."[56]

The issue of captivity entails a challenge of and a disrespect for the *Sharia* in a way that killing and the other incidents of Karbalā᾽ do not. It is an issue that equals, in its significance, the injustice that Imām al-Ḥusayn ﷺ endured and the monstrous behavior of the Umayyads.

This explains why Imām al-Ḥusayn ﷺ had insisted on taking his womenfolk with him. When his brother Muḥammad b. al-Ḥanafiyya asked him why he was taking them along, he said, "Allah has wished to see them as captives."[57]

This state of captivity had a great role in revealing the truth about Imām al-Ḥusayn's ﷺ revolt despite the prevalent idea about the

---

[56] *Al-Biḥār* 46: 108-110, and al-Muqarram, *Maqtal al-Ḥusayn* ﷺ, 377.

[57] *Al-Biḥār* 44: 364 from *Kitāb al-Malhūf*.

unjust ruler that Muʿāwiya had sought to establish.[58]

By reflecting on these five main roles that Muslim women undertook as part of the Ḥusaynī revolution, we can infer the roles of faithful women in all of Islamic history, in addition to their incomparable role in establishing the basis of human society, i.e. the family, in which they have the primary role.

All this is in addition to the intrinsic bounties that Allah ﷻ bestowed on women that allow each of them to reach perfection in her personal, individual journey within the realms of knowledge, worship, piety, sincerity toward Allah ﷻ, and generosity and giving for the sake of the flourishing of humanity as a whole. We can see all these qualities in the righteous examples in the Qur'ān, the *ḥadīth*, and Islamic history. Amongst these examples are Khadīja al-Kubrā, Sayyida Fāṭima al-Zahrā, Sayyida Zaynab ﷺ and other virtuous women.

[58] The criminal ruling regime in Iraq (Ṣaddām) also committed unjustifiable outrages and crimes and perpetrated monstrous acts that are simply beyond the pale.

At the level of moral perfection and worship, the Noble Qur'ān equates men and women, which shows us the latter's perfection at the personal and social level. This is abundantly clear from the following verse: "Indeed the Muslim men and the Muslim women, the faithful men and the faithful women, the obedient men and the obedient women, the truthful men and the truthful women, the patient men and the patient women, the humble men and the humble women, the charitable men and the charitable women, the men who fast and the women who fast, the men who guard their private parts and the women who guard, the men who remember Allah greatly and the women who remember [Allah greatly] – Allah holds in store for them forgiveness and a great reward. A faithful man or woman may not, when Allah and His Apostle have decided on a matter, have any option in their matter, and whoever disobeys Allah and His Apostle has certainly strayed into manifest error."[59]

We ask Allah ﷻ to make us, both men and women, always of the followers of Imām al-

[59] Sūrat al-Aḥzāb, 35-36.

Ḥusayn ﷺ, and we ask Him to achieve the Imām's ﷺ goals, and to make us of those who will avenge him.

www.ingramcontent.com/pod-product-compliance
Lightning Source LLC
Chambersburg PA
CBHW021449070526
44577CB00002B/328
* 9 7 8 1 9 5 6 2 7 6 0 0 8 *